Toy and Game Science

Peter Pentland and
Pennie Stoyles

CHELSEA HOUSE
PUBLISHERS
A Haights Cross Communications Company
Philadelphia

This edition first published in 2003 in the United States of America by Chelsea House
Publishers, a subsidiary of Haights Cross Communications.

Chelsea House Publishers
1974 Sproul Road, Suite 400
Broomall, PA 19008-0914

The Chelsea House world wide web address is www.chelseahouse.com

Library of Congress Cataloging-in-Publication Data

Pentland, Peter.
   Toy and game science / by Peter Pentland and Pennie Stoyles.
   p. cm. — (Science and scientists)

   Includes index.
   Summary: Describes different kinds of toys and the scientific principles that explain how
   they work.

   ISBN 0-7910-7013-1
   1. Mechanics—Juvenile literature. 2. Toys—Juvenile literature. [1. Mechanics. 2. Toys.]
   I. Stoyles, Pennie. II. Title.
   QC127.4 .P46 2003
   531—dc21

                                                        2002001285

First published in 2002 by
MACMILLAN EDUCATION AUSTRALIA PTY LTD
627 Chapel Street, South Yarra, Australia, 3141

Copyright © Peter Pentland and Pennie Stoyles 2002
Copyright in photographs © individual photographers as credited

Edited by Sally Woollett
Text design by Nina Sanadze
Cover design by Nina Sanadze
Illustrations by Pat Kermode, Purple Rabbit Productions

Printed in China

Acknowledgements
Cover: Spinning top, courtesy of Getty Images/Image Bank.

Coo-ee Picture Library, p. 16; Getty Images/Photodisc, pp. 4–5; Imageaddict, pp. 5 (top right), 26–27 bottom;
Bill Thomas/Imagen, pp. 13, 22–23, 24, 25; Legend Images, pp. 28, 29; Museum of Victoria, pp. 5 (bottom right),
6–7, 8, 9, 10–11, 12, 14, 20, 27 (top); Dale Mann/Retrospect, pp. 15, 19, 22 (left); Sporting Images, p. 17.

While every care has been taken to trace and acknowledge copyright the publisher tenders their apologies for any
accidental infringement where copyright has proved untraceable.

Contents

Glossary words

When a word is printed in bold you can look up its meaning in the Glossary on page 31.

Science terms

When a word appears like this **dissolved** you can find out more about it in the science term box located nearby.

...what is scientific about toys and games?

...what makes toys move and stop?

...why some toys make noises and others make music?

...what makes some toys fly and others float?

Did you know that all the answers have something to do with science?

The science of toys and games

The science of toys and games is about the way **forces** act on toys. It is also about the different types of **energy** that toys use and make.

Forces are needed to make some toys move or stop moving. Forces help other toys to fly, float and spin. Some toys get their energy from batteries. Others, such as musical instruments, get their energy from the person playing with the toy.

Babies and children are just like scientists who find themselves in a new situation. Like scientists, children try to find out how and why things happen. They explore their world and develop their minds and bodies using their senses. They wonder how things look, taste, feel, smell and sound. They ask a lot of questions. Toys and games help people explore the world.

Scientists

Scientists try to explain why things happen. For thousands of years they have tried to find out why things move the way they do. The answers they have found apply equally to toys, spaceships, boats, airplanes, trains, athletes and children playing.

Scientists have even taken toys into orbit around Earth to find out how toys behave in the near-weightless conditions experienced there.

There are many types of scientists, and they all have different jobs to do.

- Architects and building engineers study how to make structures stand.

- Aerospace scientists study how things fly.

- Electrical engineers study how electric motors and circuits work.

- Physicists study how objects such as toys move and what makes them stop. They also study sound and light.

In this book you will:

- explore how and why toys and games work

- meet someone who has a job working with toys

- look at some toys and find out why they move the way they do

- find out about some toys and games that work using electricity.

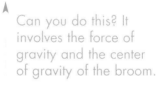

Can you do this? It involves the force of gravity and the center of gravity of the broom.

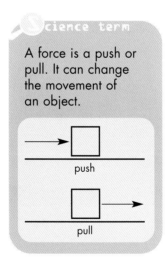

push

pull

Weird science

Some things have a center of gravity that is very hard to find. Try to find the center of gravity of a boomerang or a doughnut!

Have you ever tried to balance a broom on the tip of a finger? Why is it so hard to do?

Have you ever seen a balancing bird toy? The toy bird balances on the edge of a stand. How can it stay **horizontal** when only its beak touches the stand?

This toy relies on balance. When something is balanced it will not fall over. To understand how balanced toys work you need to know about gravity and the center of gravity.

Gravity and the center of gravity

Gravity is a **force**. It pulls objects together. It even holds the atmosphere to Earth. Scientists call the force of gravity pulling on an object its weight.

The force of gravity pulls on every part of an object. Gravity is pulling down on every part of you including your arms, legs, nose, hair and toenails. Rather than thinking about gravity pulling on every little piece of you, it is sometimes easier to think about a single point where all of the gravity seems to be concentrated. This special point is called the center of gravity. You can find the center of gravity of an object, such as a book, by balancing it on your fingertip. When the book is balanced, its center of gravity will be directly above your fingertip.

The position of the center of gravity depends on the shape of the object and how its weight is spread around the object.

How does this toy bird balance on the stand?

Balance

An object is balanced when its center of gravity is directly above the place where it touches the surface that it is standing on. The center of gravity is sometimes called the balance point. Things are easier to balance when they have a center of gravity that is close to their base and a wide area of contact with the other surface.

How the balancing bird works

The balancing bird is made of a lightweight material. It has heavy weights set into its wing tips so that its center of gravity is exactly at the tip of its beak. When the beak rests on the stand, the bird is balanced and will not tip over, even though it seems to be going against gravity.

Why is a broom hard to balance?

The center of gravity of a broom is near its head. When you try to balance a broom on your finger, the center of gravity is high and the base is small, so the broom is hard to balance.

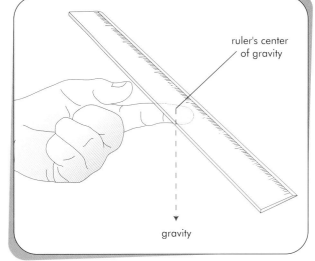

The ruler is balanced when its center of gravity is directly above the support.

ruler's center of gravity

gravity

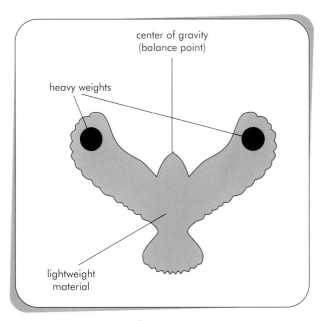

center of gravity (balance point)

heavy weights

lightweight material

▲ The weights mean that the center of gravity of the balancing bird is located in the beak.

7

Have you ever tried to make something using a saw, a hammer, nails and pieces of wood? If you have, you probably learned that you need special skills to get a good result.

Toy construction sets such as Meccano, Lego and K'Nex make it easier to build things. You do not need special equipment and skills to put them together.

Building blocks

The first construction toy a child usually plays with is a set of blocks. The thing that holds blocks together is the **friction** force between the surfaces.

Friction is caused by the roughness of the surfaces. They might look smooth, but if you looked at them under a powerful microscope you would see that they are not smooth.

You can make the force of friction bigger by using rougher surfaces or by making the amount of contact between the surfaces as big as possible.

K'Nex

This is a K'Nex model. Friction helps to hold it together.

K'Nex is a construction toy that uses a system of colored rods joined together by connectors. The ends of the rods and the arms of the connectors are specially shaped to grip onto each other. This means that more force is needed to pull them apart.

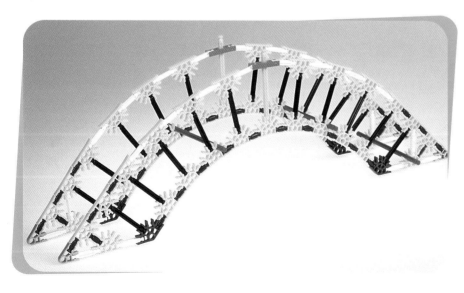

Rods of different lengths are a different color so that they are easy to find. The different colors also make following a diagram easier. The lengths of the rods are worked out so that the rods can be joined to make triangles. Triangles are very strong shapes. They cannot be easily pushed out of shape like squares or rectangles.

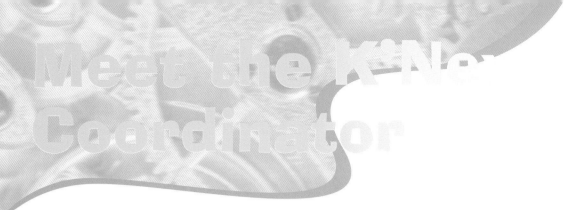

Have you ever asked yourself what it is like to work with toys and games? What sorts of jobs are there? How is it possible to get a job? What do you have to study in high school and at college?

Meet Kate Annabel

Kate Annabel has the answers to these questions. She works for Hasbro Toys as the K'Nex Events Coordinator.

Kate studied mathematics, physics, chemistry, art and English in her final year of high school. In college she studied engineering science for one year and then completed a degree in industrial design.

Kate designs and builds the K'Nex models that are used in exhibitions. She also makes models for road shows, in-store displays and TV advertisements.

She says she loves her job because it involves playing with toys all day! She finds building models to be very relaxing, and she enjoys improving the results of her work.

One task Kate had was to build a model of the International Space Station. To do this she had to search the Internet to find images of the station and to work out its **dimensions**. She then had to work out a scale for the model and figure out how to build it using K'Nex pieces. She also worked on a system with electric motors and gears to get parts of the model to move.

Every day, Kate Annabel uses the science she learned at school in her job building K'Nex models like these.

Kate is the envy of all the people she went to college with. She thinks that if you are creative and scientifically minded, you could not find a better job.

Have you ever played with small **die-cast** model cars? You can push them across the floor or along tracks. You can let them roll down ramps and race around vertical loops. You can crash them into each other. Why do they move the way they do? What stops them from moving? What happens when cars crash?

The laws of movement

Over the years scientists called physicists tried to figure out a set of rules or laws that describe how objects behave. The man who finally wrote them down is Sir Isaac Newton (1643–1727). There are three laws named after him that describe how objects move. These statements are called laws because they describe how everything in the universe behaves, from stars and planets to toys and **atoms**.

Newton's first law

Objects tend to keep doing what they are doing. If they are sitting still, they will keep sitting still until a force makes them move. If they are moving, they will keep moving at the same speed in a straight line until a force makes them speed up, slow down or change direction.

Science fact

More about Newton

Not only did Isaac Newton come up with a set of rules to describe how things move, he also made important discoveries about light, invented a type of telescope and found out about gravity. Newton also made important contributions to the studies of mathematics and astronomy.

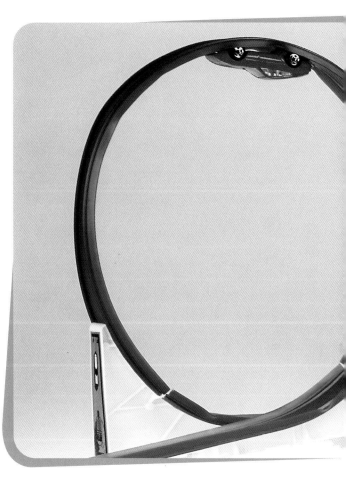

This car always obeys Newton's laws.

How the first law works

If you put a toy car on the floor it will stay there until you give it a push. If the toy car is moving it will keep going in a straight line unless you push it from the side. It will then change direction.

The car will slow down and eventually stop because the force of friction will push it in the direction opposite to the way it is moving. The car will travel farther on a hard flat floor than it will on carpet because the carpet's rough surface creates more friction.

Newton's second law

The bigger the force acting on something, the quicker that object will change its speed.

How the second law works

If you give a toy car a little push it will speed up a little bit. If you give it a hard push it will increase its speed quickly and end up going really fast.

Newton's third law

Forces work in pairs. If you push against something, it will push back against you with an equal force.

How the third law works

Imagine that a moving car crashes into a car of the same weight that is standing still. The moving car pushes the stopped car and starts it moving. At the same time the stopped car pushes back on the moving car and eventually stops it.

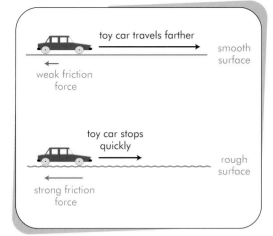

toy car travels farther
smooth surface
weak friction force

toy car stops quickly
rough surface
strong friction force

A toy car traveling across a rough surface will slow down quickly due to friction.

The red car applies a force to the stopped yellow car during a collision. This is an example of Newton's third law.

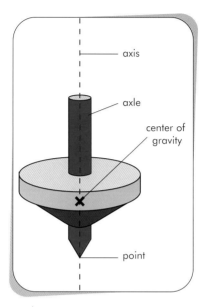

This top has a low center of gravity to make it more stable.

You have probably played with tops and yo-yos. Have you ever wondered why tops spin for so long without falling over? Why do tops fall over only when they have nearly stopped spinning? Why do yo-yos go down and then up? Why can some yo-yos spin at the end of the string?

Spinning tops

Tops have been around for thousands of years. They are made up of a disk or a regular-shaped body and an axle. The axle is a rod that passes through the top's center of gravity, and the top spins around it.

Spinning things spin around an imaginary line called an axis. In the case of a top, the axis is along the center of the axle. Think about the planet Earth spinning around its axis. It will keep on spinning at the same rate for a long time because there is little force acting on it to slow it down.

Tops stop spinning because they are slowed down by friction. Friction occurs between the point of the axle and the surface it is on. Tops spin for a long time because there is not much friction to slow them down. Friction is made as small as possible by making the tip of the axle into a sharp point and by making the tip out of hard, smooth material.

The length of time that a top spins before it tips over depends on how stable it is. Tops that have a low center of gravity are more stable and spin longer than those with a high center of gravity.

Different tops have different shapes.

Yo-yos

The yo-yo has been around for 2,500 years. It is one of the oldest toys in history. (The oldest toy is the doll.)

Simple yo-yos

The simplest kind of yo-yo is made of two disks joined by an axle. A piece of string is attached to and wrapped around the axle. When the yo-yo is used, the string unwinds from the axle and makes the disks spin. When the yo-yo gets to the end of the string, it keeps on spinning. The string winds around the axle again, causing the yo-yo to come back to the hand. Pulling up on the string will give the yo-yo enough **energy** to return to your hand.

> ### science term
> Energy is the ability of an object to do work. Energy cannot be created or destroyed, but it can be changed from one form to another.

Free-spinning yo-yos

Free-spinning yo-yos are designed for doing tricks. The string is not attached to the axle. It is looped over the axle. The yo-yo can spin in the loop until the string is jerked. Friction makes the string grip the axle and so the yo-yo rises to the hand again.

If the yo-yo starts spinning at a tipped-over angle the string will rub against one of the disks and friction will occur. This force will slow down the yo-yo and change movement energy into heat energy. Because some of the movement energy is lost, the yo-yo will often not have enough energy left to return to the hand.

The string is looped over the axle of a free-spinning yo-yo.

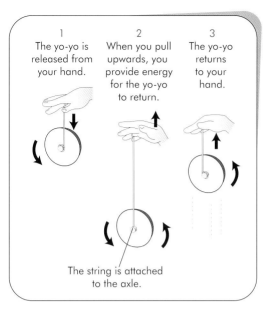

1
The yo-yo is released from your hand.

2
When you pull upwards, you provide energy for the yo-yo to return.

3
The yo-yo returns to your hand.

The string is attached to the axle.

⋏ The string is fixed to the axle of a simple yo-yo.

⋏ Pulling the string of a yo-yo gives it energy to return to your hand.

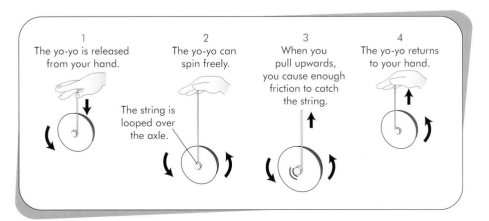

1
The yo-yo is released from your hand.

2
The yo-yo can spin freely.

The string is looped over the axle.

3
When you pull upwards, you cause enough friction to catch the string.

4
The yo-yo returns to your hand.

Science fact

Unfriendly yo-yos

The word *yo-yo* means 'come back'. It comes from the Philippines. The original people of the Philippines made and used a sharp-edged yo-yo as a weapon for more than 400 years.

Have you ever blown up a balloon and let it go before you tied the end? Why did it go whizzing around the room?

Balloons

The forces moving a balloon are acting in pairs, which is Newton's third law. When you blow air into a balloon the air pushes against the balloon and stretches it. At the same time the balloon pushes against the air inside it. When the neck of the balloon is open, the balloon pushes the air out. The balloon pushes the air in one direction and the air pushes the balloon in the opposite direction.

When the balloon is flying around, the neck of the balloon flops around, pushing the air in different directions. The air pushes against the neck and makes the balloon change its direction.

Famous scientist

Michael Faraday

Michael Faraday (1791–1867) made the first rubber balloon in 1824. He used the balloons for experiments with hydrogen gas. Faraday also made many important discoveries about electricity that led to the development of electric motors, generators and **transformers**.

Faraday also made many discoveries in chemistry. He was able to make some gases so cold that they turned into liquids. He passed an electric current through water to produce hydrogen and oxygen gases. This showed that water is made up of hydrogen and oxygen.

Balloons drive this toy car and hovercraft.

Balloon-powered toys

Some toys use balloons to drive them along. When balloon-powered toys move, they are obeying Newton's laws of movement.

Hovercrafts

A simple hovercraft toy has a flat base with a tube glued to the center of the top. A hole passes all the way through the tube and the base. A blown-up balloon is placed over the tube. The open neck of the balloon fits snugly over the tube. As air is forced from the balloon it forms a cushion of air under the base. This layer of air greatly reduces the friction between the base and the surface on which it is traveling.

With a little push, the hovercraft will travel at a steady speed in one direction. This shows Newton's first law working. An object will keep moving in one direction unless a force acts on it. When the air runs out, friction takes over and the hovercraft stops.

Rocket power

Some toy cars also use balloons to push them along. A balloon pushes air out of the back of the car through a tube. As the air is pushed in one direction, the balloon and the car are pushed in the opposite direction.

A space rocket works in the same way as a balloon. Fuel is burned in the rocket. This produces hot gases that **expand** quickly and are pushed out of an opening. As the gases are pushed out of the rocket, the rocket is pushed in the opposite direction.

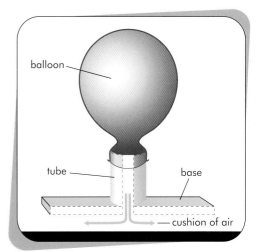

The hovercraft toy rides on a cushion of air. This means there is less friction.

Science fact

Space rockets obey Newton's laws

People used to think that rockets would not work in space because there was no air for them to push against. Luckily, Newton was right and they were wrong.

The balloon pushes the air in one direction. The air pushes the balloon and the car in the other direction.

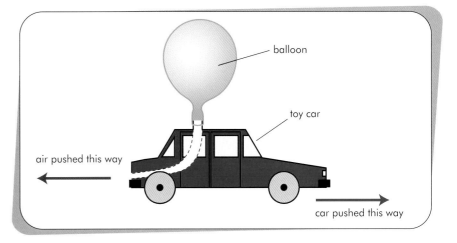

balloon

toy car

air pushed this way

car pushed this way

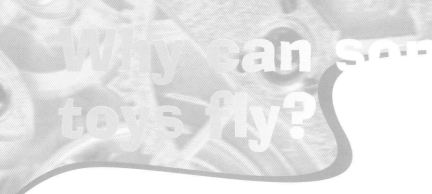

Have you ever flown a kite or thrown a plastic, Frisbee-type disk? Have you ever wondered what makes them fly? Does a kite fly in the same way as a Frisbee? What is it about air that lets heavy things like kites and Frisbees fly? The scientists who study how things fly are called aerospace scientists.

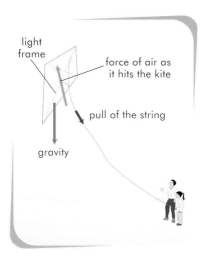

Kites have forces such as the wind and gravity acting on them.

Air

The air is a mixture of gases, mainly nitrogen and oxygen. Tiny particles of these gases are always moving. They whiz about in all directions. When the gas particles hit a surface they **push** against it and bounce off. It is the **collision** of these particles with surfaces that applies forces.

> **Science term**
>
> Air pressure is a measure of how much push the air gives to an area.

Kites

A kite is a light frame that is covered with paper or cloth. It flies in moving air and is controlled from the ground by a string.

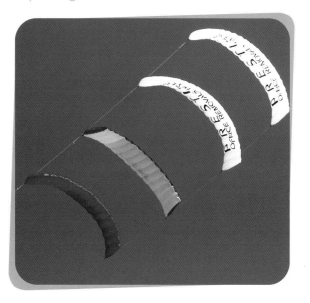

light frame

force of air as it hits the kite

pull of the string

gravity

The forces on a kite balance each other.

A flying kite is a balancing act of forces. Kites need wind to fly. The strings on a kite are attached in such a way that the kite tilts toward you when you fly it. This tilt causes the kite to push the moving air (wind) downwards. Remember that forces act in pairs. If the kite pushes the air down, then the air will push the kite up. This upward force is called lift.

There are also other forces acting on the kite. Gravity pulls the kite down. The kite is also pushed away from you in the direction that the wind is blowing. You can use the string to pull the kite through the air and to pull it down.

When the kite is flying, the upward and downward forces are balanced. So are the forces that push it away from you and pull it toward you.

Frisbees

A Frisbee is a toy shaped like a rounded disk. It is thrown and caught as a game. A Frisbee flies best when it is spinning. It acts like a top. The spinning makes the Frisbee stable and keeps it at the same angle to the air it is flying through.

Some of the Frisbee's lift can be described by the Bernoulli effect. Daniel Bernoulli (1700–1782) discovered that air moving quickly across a surface pushes less against that surface than slowly moving air does. The curved shape of the top of a Frisbee makes the air move more quickly over it. The more slowly moving air underneath pushes the Frisbee up more than the air passing over the top pushes it down. The overall effect is that the Frisbee is lifted upwards.

A Frisbee is usually slightly tilted when it flies. This means that as it flies its underside collides with more air particles. When the particles bounce off they push the Frisbee higher. In this case the Frisbee is a bit like a kite. The other forces acting on a Frisbee are gravity, which pulls it down, and air **resistance**, which slows it down.

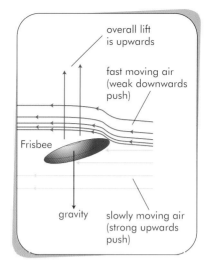

A Frisbee flies because the overall push is in an upwards direction.

Science fact

The first Frisbees

Frisbees are named after the Frisbee Baking Company in America. Students had discovered that they could throw and catch the pie tins made by the company. The first plastic Frisbee was made in 1948 by a Los Angeles building inspector named Walter Morrison and his partner, Warren Franscioni.

Frisbees usually fly at an angle to the ground.

Have you ever wondered why some things float and other things sink? Why is it that a huge ocean liner with a mass of thousands of tons will float, but a small glass marble that is lighter by far will sink? It has to do with a special force called buoyancy.

Buoyancy

There are many toys that work because of the force of buoyancy. A rubber duck in the bath, a sailing boat on a lake and an air mattress in a swimming pool all stay afloat because of this force.

Think about what happens when you get into a bath or a swimming pool. Your body pushes aside some of the water. The water pushes back on your body and lifts it up. This lifting force that acts on objects that have been put in a liquid is called buoyancy.

The buoyancy force is equal in size to the force of gravity pulling down on the water that has been pushed aside by the object.

The buoyancy force pushes this apple up while gravity and the person's mouth push it down.

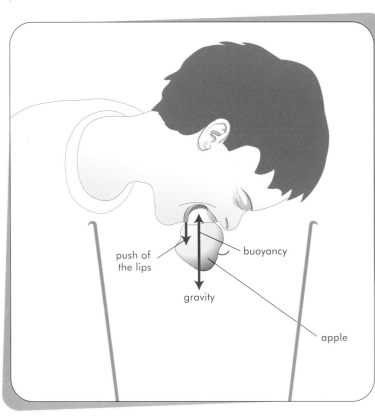

push of the lips

buoyancy

gravity

apple

Floating

Buoyancy makes things float. When you put an object like an apple into water it will sink down into the water until the buoyancy force pushing it up is equal to the gravity force pulling it down.

Bobbing for apples is a child's party game. A child puts her hands behind her back and, using only her mouth, tries to pick up an apple floating in a bowl of water. This game is difficult because the slightest push from the child's mouth will make the apple sink deeper. When the apple is pushed down, the buoyancy force pushes it up again.

Cartesian diver

Have you ever played with a Cartesian diver toy? When you squeeze the bottle containing the diver, you are changing the balance between the force of gravity pulling the diver down and the buoyancy force pushing it up.

A Cartesian diver toy has a small air-filled 'diver' that floats inside a sealed plastic bottle full of water. Water is very hard to squash, but air can be easily squashed. When the sides of the bottle are squeezed, the air inside the diver is squashed into a smaller space. Because the diver is now taking up less space, it is pushing aside less water than it did when it floated. The buoyancy force pushing the diver up is now less than the gravity force pulling it down and so the diver moves lower into the water until the forces are equal again.

When the squeeze is released, the air inside the diver fills up the larger space again and the buoyancy force becomes greater than the force of gravity. This makes the diver float back to the surface.

Sinking submarines

Submarines go under the water and rise to the surface in a similar way as the Cartesian diver. Water is pumped into ballast tanks to make the submarine sink. For the submarine to rise to the surface, the water is driven from the ballast tanks using **compressed** air.

Squeezing the 'diver' toy makes the gravity force greater than the buoyancy force. Releasing it makes the buoyancy force greater and the 'diver' rises until the forces are equal.

'diver' moves down

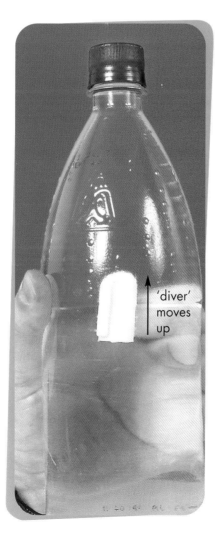

'diver' moves up

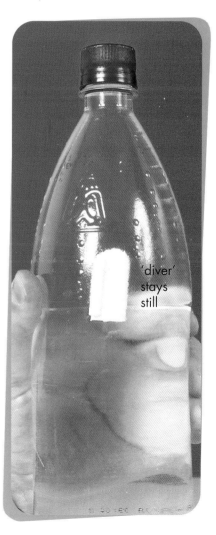

'diver' stays still

Slinky facts

• *Slinky* is a Swedish word meaning 'stealthy, sleek or sinuous'.

• Since the slinky was invented in 1945, more than 250 million have been sold.

• Making all those slinkies took almost 3 million miles (5 million kilometers) of wire. This is enough wire to wrap around Earth 126 times!

• The slinky was taken into space on a space shuttle to see if it would work in the weightless conditions of a vehicle in orbit. It did not work.

Have you ever made a slinky walk down a set of stairs? How does it work? What makes it keep going? Have you ever played with spring-driven cars? What are you doing when you wind them up? What makes them move?

What is a slinky and how does it work?

A slinky is a coil of flattened wire. Robert James invented it in 1945 to stop ship instruments from **vibrating**. The U.S. Navy did not use the invention so James's wife, Betty, decided to make it into a toy.

Potential energy is the stored energy of an object. This may be due to its shape or its position. When you place a slinky at the top of a set of stairs you give it potential energy because of its position. When a slinky 'walks' down stairs, it changes this potential energy into movement energy. This movement energy is called kinetic energy. Energy moves along the coil in a wave.

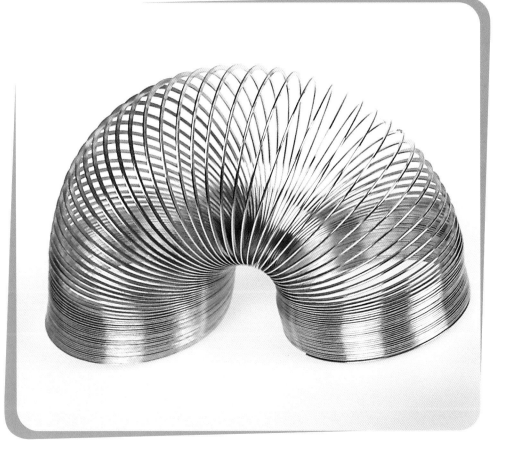

A slinky moves by changing potential energy into kinetic energy.

Wind-up cars

Many toy cars use a coiled spring to store energy. This type of energy is a slightly different type of potential energy. The energy in a wound-up spring is called potential energy because the spring will bounce back to its original shape if it is released.

When you wind up the spring of a toy car it gets tighter. A force is needed to wind up the spring. This can be done by:

- using a key
- pulling a string
- pulling the car backwards across a floor.

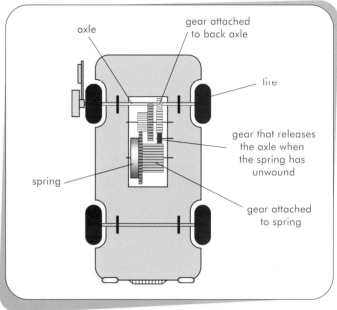

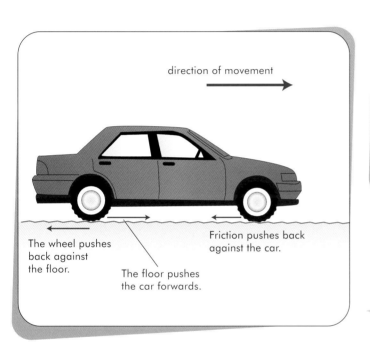

What makes the car move and stop?

The car is able to move using the energy of the spring. When you release the car from your hand the spring is able to turn its potential energy into kinetic energy. This energy is used by a gear system to turn one set of wheels on the car. The wheels push back on the floor. This makes a friction force that pushes the car forwards. The car will speed up when the spring is turning the wheels.

Once the spring has released all of its energy the car will keep moving forward until the friction between the wheels and the floor stops it. This time friction is acting in the opposite direction to the movement.

Have you ever made a tin can telephone? Do you know what a tone twirler is? Have you ever wondered how these toys work?

Sound energy

Lots of toys make noise, which is a kind of sound. Sound is a wave in air that is caused by something that is moved or vibrated. Sound needs something to travel through. Sound can be heard because it travels through air to our ears. It can also travel through liquids and through solid objects such as metal pipes and wooden tables.

The tone twirler

The tone twirler is made from a piece of tubing similar to a vacuum cleaner hose. When you swing one end of the hose around your head it makes a sound. This is because the movement of the end of the hose makes the air inside the hose vibrate.

The air inside a tone twirler vibrates when people spin it.

The hose acts in the same way as a set of panpipes. Panpipes make a sound when air is blown across the opening at the top. The air moving across the opening makes the air inside the pipe vibrate.

As you swing the tone twirler faster, the pitch of the sound jumps to higher levels. The pitch of a sound is how low or high the noise sounds. It is affected by the length of the pipe (longer pipes have a lower pitch) and how fast the air vibrates (faster vibrating air makes a higher pitched sound).

Weird science

Sound is a kind of energy. If a person talked nonstop for 3,400 years he or she would produce only enough sound energy to boil a quart (a liter) of water!

Tin can telephones

The tin can telephone is a toy you can make at home. It shows how sound can travel through string as well as through air.

When you speak you make vibrations in the air called sound waves. These are gathered by the can and make the bottom of the can vibrate. This makes the string vibrate and the sound then travels along the string to the other can. This can vibrates and makes sound waves that the other person hears.

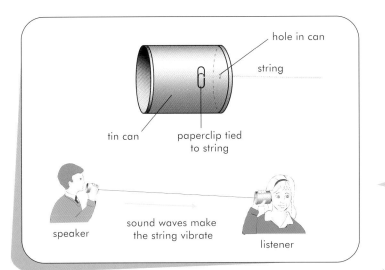

hole in can

string

tin can

paperclip tied to string

speaker

sound waves make the string vibrate

listener

One of the cans gathers sound waves from the air and makes the string vibrate. The string makes the other can vibrate. This makes sound waves in the air.

Tin can telephones are easy to make.

Try this

1 Ask an adult to remove the lids from two tin cans and clean them, making sure there are no sharp edges. Now ask them to poke a hole through the center of the bottom of each can using a hammer and nail.

2 Take a long piece of string and put the ends into the holes. Tie paperclips onto the ends of the string to prevent them pulling through the holes.

3 Hold one can, and ask a friend to hold the other. Now pull the string tight.

4 Talk through the can to the person at the other end. Listen to the other person talk.

Have you ever tried to play a real or toy musical instrument? Have you ever wondered why some sounds you made were a terrible noise and why other sounds were beautiful music? What is the difference between noise and music? How do musical instruments make sound?

Noise and music

Vibrating objects make sound. The number of times an object vibrates every second is called the frequency of the sound. People can hear sounds that have a frequency of between 20 and 20,000 vibrations a second.

The pitch of a musical note is how high or low the note is. Low notes have a small frequency. High notes have a large frequency.

A noise is a jumble of different sounds mixed together in a random way. A musical note is different from noise because it has an exact frequency. For example, somebody singing the musical note middle C is making 256 vibrations a second.

Musical toys

Musical toys are simple versions of real instruments. All musical instruments have a part that vibrates and a part that makes the sound louder.

Tin whistles

You play a tin whistle by blowing into it through a specially shaped mouthpiece. This makes the air in the tube vibrate. Long, wide tubes make low notes. Short, narrow tubes make high notes. More of the tube is sealed by covering more holes, starting from the top. You can make the tin whistle sound louder by blowing harder.

Weird science

The great opera singer Enrico Caruso was said to be able to shatter a crystal wineglass by singing just the right note as loudly as he could. This was possible because the sound of his voice would make the glass vibrate. If he sang the right note, the vibrations of the glass would get bigger and bigger until the crystal fell apart.

This trick does not work with an ordinary glass.

The mouthpiece of a tin whistle makes the air in the tube vibrate when you blow through it.

Xylophones

When you play a xylophone, the parts that vibrate are bars of metal. The different size and thickness of each bar means that each bar makes a sound with a different frequency. Long, wide and thick bars make low notes with small frequencies. Short, narrow and thin bars make high notes with large frequencies. You can make a toy xylophone produce a louder noise by hitting the bars harder.

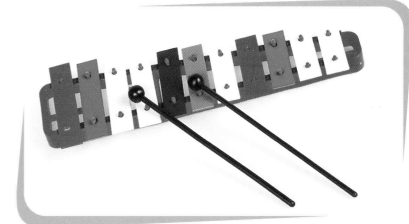

Guitars

You play a guitar by making the strings vibrate. Long and thick strings make low notes. Thin strings make high notes. You can make a string shorter by pressing it against the fret board on the neck of the guitar. This will make a higher note. You can also make the note of a string higher by making it tighter. The tightness of the strings is adjusted by turning the pegs at the end of the fret board. The guitar's sound box makes the sound louder.

The metal bars of a xylophone vibrate when you hit them.

The sound box of a guitar makes the sound of a note louder.

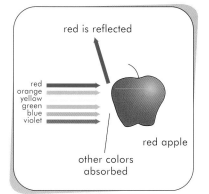

A red apple looks red because it reflects red light.

Have you ever wondered how a kaleidoscope makes colored patterns? Have you ever used a 3-D viewer? Have you ever wondered how some toys use light? To understand how these toys work you have to know a bit about how light behaves.

Light

Light travels in straight lines. The way that light travels is in the form of a wave. The color of light depends on the length of its wave. Red has the longest wavelength and violet has the shortest wavelength.

Some objects give off light. Others absorb it, reflect it or let it pass through. The color of an object depends on what colors it absorbs and what colors it reflects or lets through. A red apple mainly reflects red light and absorbs the other colors.

Science fact

Clever eyes

Humans can tell the difference between about 10 million different colors.

Kaleidoscopes

A kaleidoscope is a tube containing two mirrors along its length. At the opposite end to the eyepiece it has a number of colored see-through shapes that move around in front of a window made of a translucent material. Translucent materials let light through but you cannot see through them.

When light enters through the translucent material it is scattered in different directions. The light then passes through the colored shapes and is reflected from mirror to mirror as it passes along the tube. By the time the light reaches the eyepiece, the mirrors have multiplied the images of the colored shapes many times. You see this as a colored pattern.

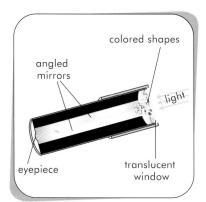

Light reflects off two mirrors several times in a kaleidoscope before it reaches your eyes.

Kaleidoscopes make beautiful patterns.

26

How do people see?

You have two eyes sitting at the front of your head. Each eye forms a slightly different image of the scene you are looking at. The images are sent as electrical signals through your optic nerves to the brain. Your brain puts the signals together, which means you can understand what you see. You can also judge the length, width and distance away that an object is. These three things are called dimensions, and being able to see all of them is called viewing in three dimensions, or 3-D.

When you look through a 3-D viewer each eye is actually seeing a different image.

3-D viewers

The disk of a 3-D viewer has pairs of pictures of a scene taken from slightly different angles. The pairs of pictures are on opposite sides of the disk. When you look at the disk through the viewer each eye gets a different view of a scene. The brain processes these views and makes a 3-D picture in your mind.

Have you ever played the magnetic fishing game? In this game, players try to catch a paper fish that has a paperclip on its nose. They do this using a weak magnet on a piece of string that is tied to the end of a rod. What is it about a magnet that attracts it to some metals and not others?

Magnets

Have you ever used a bar magnet? A bar magnet is a special bar of steel that attracts iron. Magnets do not attract all metals, only those that contain the metals iron, cobalt or nickel.

Magnetic poles

Bar magnets are strongest at the ends. The ends are called poles. When a magnet is hung from a piece of cotton thread its ends will line up in a north–south direction. The end that points to the north is called the north-seeking or N pole. The other end is the south-seeking or S pole.

The N poles and S poles of magnets attract each other. Poles that are the same repel each other. So an S pole repels other S poles and an N pole repels other N poles.

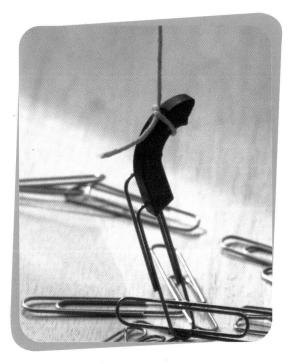

Magnetic fishing game

When a person playing the magnetic fishing game catches a paperclip fish, they need to lift it into the air. Paperclips are made of steel, which contains iron. When the paperclip is being lifted the magnetic force attracting the paperclip to the magnet is bigger than the force of gravity pulling the paperclip down. If the player pulls the magnet up too quickly, the fish will fall off.

The magnetic fishing game. A magnet attracts the iron found in steel paperclips.

Electric t

Have you ever played games that use electricity? Did you ever wonder what electricity is? 'Operation' is a simple game that uses electricity. To understand how this game works you first need to know some of the science of electricity. The scientists who study this science are called electrical engineers.

Electricity

Electricity is a form of energy. It can be produced by power stations, and it can be stored in batteries.

An electric circuit is an unbroken pathway that will allow electricity to flow through it. It has a source of electricity, such as a battery or a power point, which pushes the electricity around the circuit. It also includes the appliance that will use the electricity, such as a lightbulb. The appliance turns the electrical energy into other forms of energy. A lightbulb turns electrical energy into heat and light. A buzzer turns electrical energy into sound energy.

'Operation'

The game 'Operation' is an example of a simple electric circuit. It tests the steadiness of the players' hands. Players try to remove plastic organs from a patient using metal tweezers that are connected by wire to one side of a battery. The picture of the patient is mounted on a metal plate that is connected to the other side of the battery. A lightbulb and a buzzer are connected between the battery and the metal plate. Plastic organs sit in holes in the plate. If the tweezers touch the metal that surrounds the hole the electric circuit is completed. A bulb lights up and a buzzer sounds.

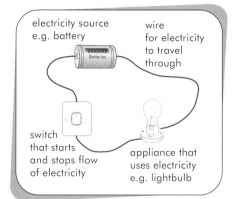

electricity source e.g. battery

wire for electricity to travel through

switch that starts and stops flow of electricity

appliance that uses electricity e.g. lightbulb

An electric circuit contains a source and an appliance.

Science fact

Conductors and insulators

• Materials that let electricity pass through them are called conductors. Metals like copper are good conductors.

• Insulators are materials that stop electricity from passing through them. Nonmetals like plastic and wood are good insulators.

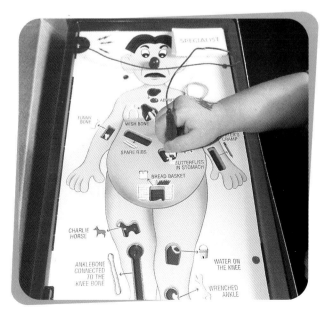

Players complete the circuit when they touch the metal sides of the holes in the 'Operation' game.

This timeline shows some important toy science events. See if you can imagine some of the things that might happen in toy science in the future.

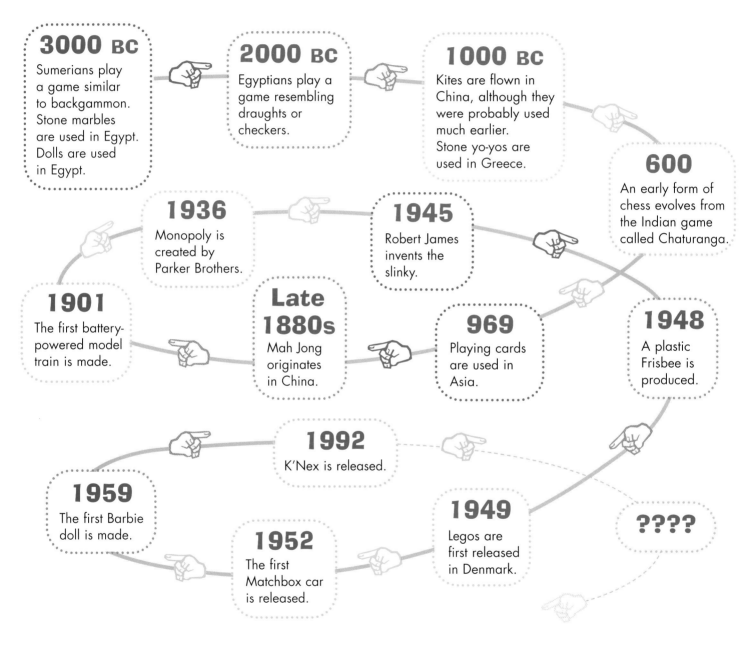

3000 BC
Sumerians play a game similar to backgammon. Stone marbles are used in Egypt. Dolls are used in Egypt.

2000 BC
Egyptians play a game resembling draughts or checkers.

1000 BC
Kites are flown in China, although they were probably used much earlier. Stone yo-yos are used in Greece.

600
An early form of chess evolves from the Indian game called Chaturanga.

1936
Monopoly is created by Parker Brothers.

1945
Robert James invents the slinky.

1901
The first battery-powered model train is made.

Late 1880s
Mah Jong originates in China.

969
Playing cards are used in Asia.

1948
A plastic Frisbee is produced.

1992
K'Nex is released.

1959
The first Barbie doll is made.

1952
The first Matchbox car is released.

1949
Legos are first released in Denmark.

????

What are scientists working on now?

⊙ Scientists are developing dolls that can have their personalities programmed on computer chips.

Glossary

atoms	tiny particles that combine to make up all things, be they solid, liquid or gas
collision	bumping of two or more objects together
compressed	pressed closely together, forced into a smaller space than usual
die-cast	made by pouring liquid metal into a mold
dimensions	the length, width and height of an object
energy	the ability of an object to do work. Energy cannot be created or destroyed, but it can be changed from one form to another
expand	increase in size
forces	pushes or pulls. Forces can change the movement or shape of an object
horizontal	in line with the ground
resistance	the act of one object or force working against another
transformers	equipment that transfers electrical energy
vibrating	shaking from side to side

Index